Circular Walks
on
Eastern Dartmoor

Liz Jon

OBELISK PUBLICATIONS

OTHER DARTMOOR TITLES ...

Ten Family Walks on Dartmoor, Sally and Chips Barber
Six Short Pub Walks on Dartmoor, Sally and Chips Barber
Walks in the Shadow of Dartmoor, Denis McCallum
Walks in Tamar and Tavy Country, Denis McCallum
The Great Walks of Dartmoor, Terry Bound
Walks in the Chagford Countryside, Terry Bound
The A to Z of Dartmoor Tors, Terry Bound
Under Sail through South Devon and Dartmoor, Raymond B Cattell
The Great Little Dartmoor Book, Chips Barber
The Great Little Chagford Book, Chips Barber
Dark and Dastardly Dartmoor, Sally and Chips Barber
Weird and Wonderful Dartmoor, Sally and Chips Barber
The Templer Way, Derek Beavis
The Dartmoor Mountain Bike Guide, Peter Barnes
Beautiful Dartmoor, Chips Barber
Cranmere Pool – The First Dartmoor Letterbox, Chips Barber
Diary of a Dartmoor Walker, Chips Barber
Diary of a Devonshire Walker, Chips Barber
The Teign Valley of Yesteryear, Parts I and II, Chips Barber
Princetown of Yesteryear, Parts I and II, Chips Barber
Widecombe – A Visitor's Guide, Chips Barber

We have over 150 Devon titles. For a full list of current books, please contact us at Obelisk Publications, 2 Church Hill, Pinhoe, Exeter, Devon, EX4 9ER or telephone (01392) 468556.

To Bella

Faithful Friend

Plate Acknowledgements
All drawings by Jane Reynolds
Photographs on pages 5 (middle), 16 (middle), 25 and 26 by Liz Jones
All other photographs by Chips Barber
Sketch maps drawn from an out-of-copyright source

First published in 1997 by
Obelisk Publications, 2 Church Hill, Pinhoe, Exeter, Devon
Designed by Chips and Sally Barber
Typeset by Sally Barber
Printed in Great Britain by
The Devonshire Press Ltd, Torquay, Devon

CONTENTS

STEPS BRIDGE – HELTOR

Distance:	*Approx. $2^{3}/_{4}$ miles*
Time:	*Allow $1^{1}/_{2}$ – 2 hours*
Map:	*OS Landranger 191; OS Outdoor Leisure 28*
Start reference:	*SX802884*
Terrain:	*Woodland and field paths; steep climbs*
Nearest town:	*Moretonhampstead*
Parking:	*Steps Bridge car park (free)*
Refreshments:	*Steps Bridge Inn (Seasonal)*

Cross the road to enter Bridford Wood, turning right up the track for the youth hostel. Follow the path indicated Heltor Farm and Westcott, which climbs steadily through this deciduous woodland. The woodland floor is massed with field woodrush, primroses, lesser celandine and bilberry, providing a colourful relief in season.

The path climbs steadily, until a ladder stile into a field is reached. Go straight ahead from this stile to a gate where the path is again signposted, but take a moment to enjoy the view from this point – Dunsford is easily located. Keeping the hedgerow on the left, follow the path through the fields, and Heltor Rock soon dominates the view. Emerging onto a stony track keep the same course to descend to Heltor Farm, bearing left to pass in front of the farmhouse and arrive at a metalled lane.

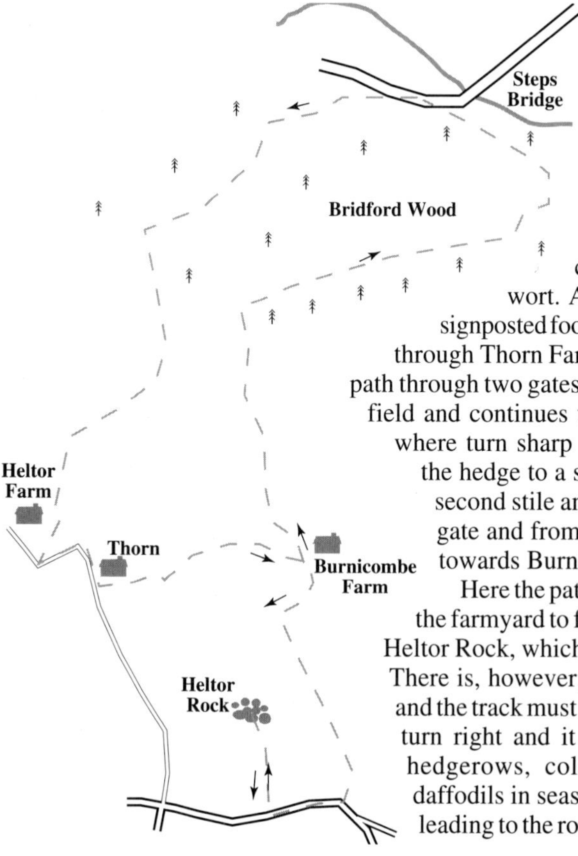

Turn left along this lane and climb between high hedges full of foxgloves, cranesbill, yarrow and pennywort. At the top of the hill, take the signposted footpath on the left to Burnicombe through Thorn Farm and follow the waymarked path through two gates; the path now bears left into a field and continues to the far corner of the field, where turn sharp right and continue alongside the hedge to a stile. Walk straight ahead to a second stile and enter a field. Bear right to a gate and from the gate continue straight on towards Burnicombe Farm.

Here the path divides again. Walk through the farmyard to follow the track uphill towards Heltor Rock, which is easily seen from the track. There is, however, no access through the fields and the track must be followed to the minor road; turn right and it is a short distance between hedgerows, colourful with primroses and daffodils in season, to reach the stile and path leading to the rock. From here there are superb

views across the surrounding countryside and Blackingstone Rock sits on the horizon.

A story connects the two granite monoliths of Blackingstone and Heltor, which apparently were not to be seen at one time; on the hills where these Rocks are placed, King Arthur and the Evil One once stood their ground, heaving quoits at each other – the Devil lost this encounter. Where the quoits fell they changed into rocks and so the masses we now look upon were formed. Believe it if you will! The name Hel Tor, however, does not reflect this contest – Hel means high.

From the Rock, retrace the outward route to Burnicombe Farm and from there follow the signed path to Steps Bridge and continue to a gate into a field. A small stream flows away to the right; follow the path until it ends abruptly beside a large holly bush and cross the stream to follow the path back into Bridford Wood.

Descend the steep path until a signpost is reached on the right indicating "Footpath Only No Horses". Take this path which runs along the top edge of the woodland. It may be noticed that the plants in this area of the wood vary from those lower down; look out for wood anemones, violets, wood sorrel, bluebells, foxgloves, dog's mercury and wild

Heltor Rock

garlic. Mosses of all kinds grow around the trees and banks, including stag's horn clubmoss and common hair moss. As well as the mosses and flowers, there are lichen and bracket fungi growing here, particularly the birch bracket. Make quiet progress and there is every possibility of seeing a group of Roe deer, browsing through the trees.

Continue on this path until it ends at a junction with a bridlepath signposted both left and right; turn left and continue descending. Another path joins at an acute angle from the right; turn down this path and again descend as the path swings left.

Stay on this path, lined by oak, birch, sycamore and hazel, beneath which grow wood rush, wood anemones, bluebells, wood cow-wheat, ferns and mosses. Gradually the River Teign can be heard and seen as the path passes above the fast-flowing river.

The descent is gradual and the path emerges onto the road opposite the Steps Bridge Inn. Turn left to return to the car park.

MORETONHAMPSTEAD – MARDON DOWN VIA PEPPERDON AND BLACKINGSTONE

Distance:	*Approx. 5½ miles*
Time:	*Allow 2½ – 3 hours*
Map:	*OS Outdoor Leisure 28*
Start reference:	*SX754859*
Terrain:	*Rough tracks, field paths and country lanes; some climbs*
Parking:	*Station Road car park (free)*
Refreshments:	*Several places in Moretonhampstead*

Turn right into Station Road to pass the site of the old railway station, closed in 1959, which is now a haulage yard.

The author and keen walker, Miss Hannah Cox O'Neill, lived at No. 2 Courtenay Terrace in Station Road from 1900 to 1915; she is buried at North Bovey.

Pass the Old Toll House on the left and shortly the Wray Brook is crossed. Part of the railway bridge still stands to the right of this well-used road, where wide verges offer refuge from the traffic. Before another bridge over the Wray Brook, turn left up the track to Budleigh Farm; the path is signposted to Pepperdon Down. Follow the track upwards, bearing left in front of the house and passing to the left of 'The Cottage'. Shortly an arrow indicates the path turns right behind the cottage and continues onto a grassy track leading uphill to the rear of the farmhouse.

This track is bordered by sycamore, elder, oak, holly and hazel and in season there are many wildflowers here including campion, foxgloves, green alkanet, hedge woundwort and spear thistles. Views are glimpsed through the trees and the track becomes a path as it enters a field; wood cudweed, pearlwort and self-heal may be found in the short grass here. Keep along the bottom edge of the field, continuing on a roughly ESE course to a stile bearing waymarkings.

In summer the path disappears into a dense forest of bracken, before emerging into another rough field. Once again, keep along the bottom edge of the field and at the corner, turn right through two granite gateposts with waymarkings. Pass into mixed deciduous woodland, where the ground is massed with pink purslane in late spring and summer, and follow the line of the wall to the right for approximately 100 yards before swinging upwards (ESE) through the bracken; the path is indicated by waymarkings on the trees, although this may not be easy to see when the bracken is high. Keep on a course which moves upwards away from the wall, until a stile is reached and the path enters a field. Into the field take a SE course

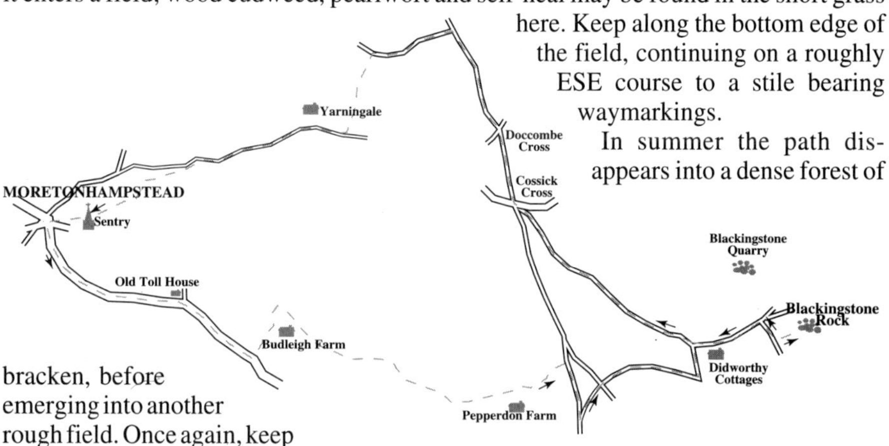

across the corner to a point where the path is signposted along the edge of the field.

From the top of Blackingstone Rock

Walk up the field to a ladder stile, but before continuing, spare a few moments to enjoy the splendid view. Climb through two more fields and exit via a ladder stile onto a minor road at the edge of Pepperdon Down. Turn right along the road for a few yards, then turn left onto a wide track across rough ground which leads to another road; here turn right. There are wonderful views from this road and Haytor Rocks and Houndtor can be picked out easily on a clear day.

Take the next turning left onto a narrow unsigned lane opposite a signpost, which indicates Hennock straight on. The large mass of Blackingstone Rock comes into view quite soon – its shape is reminiscent of a petrified cottage loaf! When the T-junction at Didworthy is reached, turn right uphill and shortly after the entrance to Blackingstone Quarry, take the first turning on the right. Walk a few yards along this road to find the path on the left which leads to Blackingstone Rock.

The path goes around the Rock to steps, complete with handrails, which were put up in the 1870s. The steps are very narrow and it is extremely windy atop the Rock on a blustery day. However, the views from the top are breathtaking – to the NW, in the far distance, is Yes Tor on Okehampton Common; west of the Rock is Fernworthy Forest, whilst in the middle distance is the ridge of Hamel Down to the south-west; Hound Tor and Haytor Rocks should be easily distinguished. Look to the NE and pick out Hel Tor Rock in the near distance.

A sorry story attaches to Blackingstone. It was recorded by Miss Bidder, the daughter of Mr George Parker Bidder (of whom more later). It concerns three croaking ravens who lived at Blackingstone and a woman with a baby who lived at nearby Brennan (recorded on the OS map as Brinning). The mother, on hearing the bells ringing for Moreton Fair, was unable to resist the temptation to attend. She left the baby unprotected on the moor to play and collect "urts" (whortleberries), whilst she hastened to the Fair. On her way she saw the three ravens fly overhead from Blackingstone. She called to them, "Where be you a-goin' to, ravens cruel?" They replied, "Up to Brennan! Up to Brennan!" She had not gone far before this event repeated itself. As she was at the outskirts of Moreton, once again she saw three ravens and again repeated her question and received the same answer. It was not until the evening that she returned home; there was no baby's voice to welcome her – all that remained was a heap of well-picked white bones.

Leave Blackingstone Rock and rejoin the road to return to Didworthy Cottages. At the junction keep straight on between high hedges, containing honeysuckle, elder and rowan. Once more there are views to be enjoyed and Mardon Down is seen ahead.

At Cossick Cross, cross the road to take the lane to Mardon Down and Clifford Bridge. This narrow lane is edged by a granite wall, on which grows stonecrop, wall-pennywort, polypody ferns and sheep's bit scabious. Keep on this road to arrive at the edge of

Mardon Down, where turn left (W) along the road. Walk along the edge of the Down for about 500 yards to locate a path on the left (S), as gradually views across southern Dartmoor open up. The path descends through the bracken and gorse to a stile with a small gate alongside.

Follow this path downhill, to exit through another gate onto a metalled track. Turn right and then bear left at Yarningale onto a grassy track; keep to the right to enter a narrow footpath between high hedgerows. After approximately a quarter of a mile the way divides; fork left (WSW) to follow the path into the Sentry (or Sanctuary) field, and from here make for the church.

Within the church porch are three memorial stones, which were originally in the churchyard. Two of these stones are to French prisoners of war, captured during the Napoleonic Wars and sent to Princetown prison. French Officers were allowed parole, enabling them to live in nearby towns; Moretonhampstead was one of these towns. These two Officers, Louis Ambroise Quantin and Arnaud Aubry, died before peace was declared.

Inside the church, there is a memorial plaque to Moretonhampstead's most famous son, George Parker Bidder (1806 – 1878). He was born in a cottage in New Street on 14th June, the son of a stonemason. He received no formal education but was able, before the age of seven, to calculate arithmetical problems; at this time he could hardly read and did not understand terms such as feet and inches when asked to calculate how many inches in a square foot. However, with the aid of explanation he could quickly answer any problem; his father exploited this remarkable gift, travelling the country with his son and putting on exhibitions. At the age of eight he appeared before Queen Charlotte at Windsor Castle, where he duly answered correctly a problem put to him by the Queen. Due to wealthy benefactors who recognised his potential, he was able to attend Camberwell Grammar School from 1817 to 1818. He then attended Edinburgh University, which he left in 1824. He spent a year with the Ordnance Survey Office before being engaged as a Civil Engineer. In 1833 he superintended the construction of Blackwall Wharf, and in 1834 he joined forces with Robert and George Stephenson, whom he had met whilst at Edinburgh. He was to play a large part in the development of railway communications in Britain and was a founder of the Electric Telegraph Company.

His chief works are the construction of Lowestoft Harbour and the Victoria Docks at North Woolwich, London. He travelled countrywide, but never forgot his Devon roots, becoming President of the Devonshire Association in 1860; he was also President of the Institute of Civil Engineers from 1860 to 1861. He died at Dartmouth on 20th September.

In the churchyard, the granite memorial cross to those killed in the 1914–18 War was made at Blackingstone Quarry.

Into Fore Street, pass the school and after the Bowring Library (L), turn left and keep straight on to return to the car park.

MORETONHAMPSTEAD – NORTH BOVEY

Distance:	*Approx. 4½ miles*
Time:	*Allow 2½ – 3 hours*
Map:	*OS Outdoor Leisure 28*
Start reference:	*SX752860*
Terrain:	*Country lanes, field paths and tracks; some climbs*
Parking:	*Car park, Court Street (free)*
Refreshments:	*Several places in Moretonhampstead; Ring O'Bells, North Bovey*

Turn left to descend Court Street towards the Square. Go right (S) into Pound Street and after a short distance the road forks; bear left (S) onto a quiet country lane, where the verges are massed with wild flowers, including stitchwort, lesser celandine, cranesbill, white and red deadnettle and garlic mustard in season. Initially, there are views to Hingston Down but later the hedgerows close in.

The Wadley Brook is crossed and the road climbs. The flora changes as the hedges turn to stone walls and wall-pennywort, ivy-leaved toadflax, ferns and liverworts are found. There is even a lilac naturalised in the hedge and growing profusely. On arrival at Brinning, notice the magnificent horse chestnut trees and the attractive garden.

A short distance up the hill from Brinning, leave the road and take the signposted footpath on the left to North Bovey via Narramore and Fursdon. After the stile keep to the left of the field and follow the well defined path leading SE. There is a brief view to Hingston Down.

Cross a small stream and continue alongside the hedge through two fields; cross a track and keep the same course across the next two fields. Emerging into a small clump of trees, bear right to a stile into another field. Walk diagonally left across this field to a

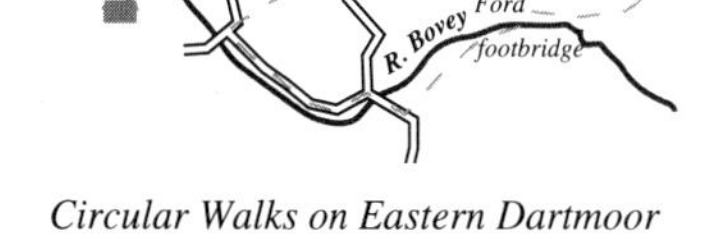

stile and the driveway to Narramore Farm. Turn right to the road, which cross to take the track indicated North Bovey via Fursdon. There are good views from this point to Easdon Down on the edge of the moor, and the banks alongside the track are colourful with primroses, violets, ground ivy, polypody ferns and honeysuckle in the spring and early summer.

The track ends abruptly just prior to a barn and turns sharp right over a stile. Go straight across the field to another stile and cross the farm track; through the gate ahead bear left (SW) to a ladder stile. Keep a south-westerly course across this field to another gate and a footpath sign. From here the twin humps of Haytor Rocks are clearly seen, Bowerman's nose stands out on Hayne Down and ahead is Hamel Down. Continue on the same course across this field to a slip bar stile where there is a small amount of water to negotiate each side of the stile – these are tributaries to Dickford Water, which is a stream flowing into the River Bovey.

Follow a SW course across this next field to a stile. Notice the area of soft rush growing here, creating a dark green patch in the field; also to be found from March to June is lady's smock or cuckoo flower. Both these plants are an indication of moist ground. Keep alongside the left-hand hedge in the next field to a stile, and emerge into a lane rich in wild flowers during the season. Pink purslane (flowering April–July) grows here in abundance enjoying the damp shade. Follow the lane downwards to another stile and exit onto a wide track, where turn right.

After a short distance turn left across a narrow footbridge over the River Bovey, or walk on to the ford and cross via the large stepping stones. Continue along the track which emerges onto a minor road, bearing right over the bridge to cross the River Bovey once more.

Turn left (NW) along the road to Blackaller; the river banks here are always full of colour – snowdrops in early spring and later there are green alkanet, pink purslane and anemones to be seen. At Blackaller bear right and turn immediately right up the path indicated to North Bovey village and church. A steep climb, but a short one, arrives at the gate into the churchyard.

This church was fortunate to have the services of the Reverend Thornton for 50 years. He came to North Bovey in February 1866 and recorded in the diary he kept (later published in two volumes) that his "new parishioners were very turbulent people" and that "they flung crockery and stones at one another, and one actually leaned out of a window, pistol in hand, and threatened the life of a policeman". In their defence he also records that "they were as generous as they were fierce". Visitors are assured of a more appropriate welcome now!

The late Viscount Hambleden financed restoration of the church in 1916–1918. He lived at what is now called the Manor House Hotel, which will be seen on the return route to Moretonhampstead.

The Reverend Thornton and his wife are buried near to the south porch and close by, near the lych gate, lies Hannah Cox O'Neill (1834–1915), a close friend of the Thorntons. She lived at Moretonhampstead from 1900 to 1915, popularising Devon in her books entitled *Told in the Dimpsies* and *Devonshire Idylls*. An enthusiastic walker, she instigated the provision of two seats along the North Bovey road, for the benefit of wayfarers.

A glance back on leaving the churchyard will reveal that the church clock bears the words "Thy Kingdom Come" instead of numbers. The twisted yew to the left of the lych gate is at least 300 years old. Outside the gate turn left along the road to pass beside the village green.

The village cross on the edge of the green was torn down during the Civil War, when the cross was a hated symbol. This present cross was found nearby and re-erected by the then curate, Reverend R. P. Jones, in 1829; however, this is not the original cross. The splendid oaks on the green were nearly all planted to commemorate important or special occasions and a granite tablet at the foot of each tree denotes whether this was a Royal Coronation or Jubilee or the ending of the First World War. The old village pump also stands on the green and this was once the only source of water for many of the 17th and 18th century cottages.

Follow the road north towards Moretonhampstead and when 'Pound Rocks' is reached, bear left. After approximately 200 yards a stile is reached on the right and the footpath crosses a field. From the stile look back across the valley to see the Manor House Hotel.

This Manor House was the seat of the first Viscount Hambleden (William Frederick Danvers Smith), who was the son of the Rt. Hon. William Henry Smith (whose father was the founder of W. H. Smith & Son). In 1880 William Smith purchased more than 5,000 acres of land and properties in the parishes of North Bovey (including North Bovey village), Moretonhampstead and Lustleigh. The Manor House, completed in 1907, was built by the first Lord Hambleden. William Smith would have been created Viscount Hambleden, but died before the title could be conferred on him.

Take a northerly course across the next two fields. Turn left on entering the following field and pass through a gate into another field; keep straight across this field to a stile and exit onto a minor road. Cross the road and take the track signposted County Road for Moretonhampstead. The track is edged by high hedges but there is a view ahead. Into a field, keep the hedge to the left, following the yellow waymarkings as the path continues along a cart-track through fields. Views open up over Moretonhampstead and upwards to Hingston Down. Emerging onto a metalled lane, the path is indicated left.

After a few yards the path turns right again and descends through two more fields. Bear right at the bottom of the second field and climb a stile into Killerton Lane. The water running beside this lane is a tributary of the Wadley Brook.

Exit onto the B3212 (Court Street) at the edge of Moretonhampstead and turn right along the road to return to the car park.

ILSINGTON – LENDA VIA LOUNSTON

Distance:	*Approx. 5 miles*
Time:	*Allow 2½ – 3 hours*
Map:	*OS Outdoor Leisure 28*
Start reference:	*SX785763*
Terrain:	*Rough tracks, woodland paths, minor lanes; some climbs*
Nearest town:	*Bovey Tracey*
Parking:	*Ilsington*
Refreshments:	*Carpenter's Arms, Ilsington*

Leave the village walking roughly SE along Old Town Hill; this becomes a narrow lane bordered by high hedges of hazel, blackthorn and holly, which are host to hogweed, chervil, cranesbill and hedge bedstraw. There are snatches of a view across Silver Wood through the hedge to the right.

After a short distance footpath signs are reached both sides of the road. Take the footpath on the left through Ilsington Wood, and follow the path straight ahead through this mixed woodland of hazel, sycamore, oak and birch; common hair moss, wood sorrel and bluebells are abundant here in season.

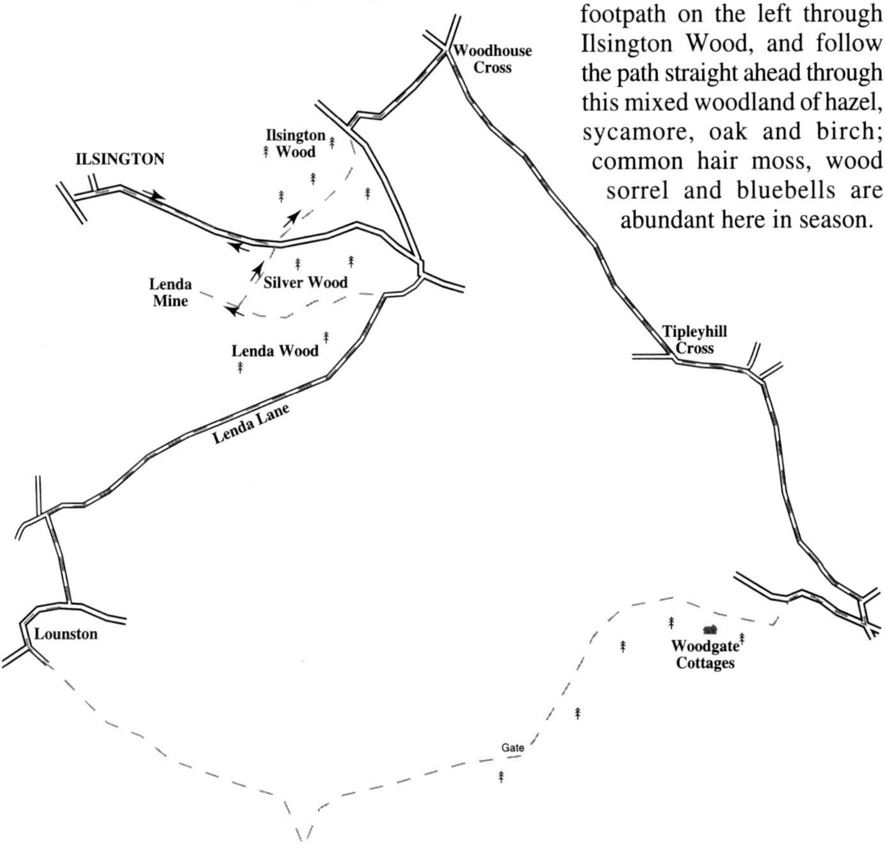

Leave this woodland via a stile and steps onto a road, which cross onto a minor lane, shortly crossing a bridge over the Liverton Brook; growing along the water's edge are fine-leaved water dropwort and pink purslane. Climb steadily, enjoying the view across fields to the right and appreciate the full glory of the woodland just traversed.

When Woodhouse Cross is reached, turn right into Tipleyhill Lane, which is a rough stony track. Initially there are splendid views to be enjoyed before the dense hedges, colourful with herb robert, chervil, black bryony, foxgloves, cleavers and bedstraw, become too high. A gateway is reached on the right and here pause a while to enjoy the magnificent views across fields and trees to Haytor Rocks.

After Tipleyhill Cross, the surface becomes a metalled lane and gradually descends. Ahead the town of Bovey Tracey is seen and the track bends sharply right. Leave the metalled lane and fork right onto another unmade track, passing between high hedges. Initially level, the track descends to pass cottages and emerge onto a minor lane. Turn right, then right again along a narrow road.

Once again the Liverton Brook is crossed, after which turn sharp left onto a track leading to Woodgate Cottages. Pass the cottages and turn sharp right onto the signposted footpath to Lower Lounston, which runs behind the cottages. Rora Wood is entered, where can be found growing such plants as wood cow-wheat, yellow pimpernel, wood avens and hard ferns, flourishing in the cool damp shade alongside the brook which runs through the woodland.

The path through the trees turns abruptly to the right and crosses the brook. Pass through a gate, where the way is signposted and waymarked, and enter a large field. Follow a westerly course to arrive at the top left hand corner of this field. Early purple orchids may be found growing here in the late spring and early summer months in the damp area at the bottom of this field. A steady climb provides a good reason for stopping at the top of this field to admire the view once more.

Pass through the gate in the corner of the field and walk straight ahead along the narrow path to join a wider track, where bear right to continue towards Lower Lounston. This route offers splendid scenery, including views to Haytor Rocks and Saddle Tor.

The track surface improves as Lower and Great Lounston are reached and the track joins a minor road. Bear right uphill and as the road levels, take the unmade track on the left. At a junction of tracks, take that on the right, which descends – this is Lenda Lane.

Follow this stony track between high hedges full of foxgloves, cranesbill, speedwell and stitchwort, all attracting butterflies during the summer months. Eventually, the edge of Lenda Wood is reached; continue to descend the lane until a wide stony track is reached on the left, which is indicated as a permitted path – Lenda Wood is privately owned, the owner having given permission for access. There is no legal right of way.

This track passes a large disused quarry to the left and climbs gently through the hazel, ash, holly and birch trees; once again yellow pimpernel and pink purslane can be found and there are many ferns on the woodland floor. Cross the small stream and ascend.

The spoil heaps are passed to the left of this track, which leads to the ruined mine buildings. They are now smothered in vegetation and the brick chimney stack is just discernible above its covering of ivy. The mine is over 300 years old and was last worked in the 19th century, closing in 1861. In its heyday it produced lead and tin as well as silver.

Just prior to the ruined buildings, a path on the right leads upwards into the trees. Keep climbing to arrive once more at Old Town Hill, opposite the path taken on the outward route. Turn left along the road to Ilsington.

HOUND TOR – SMALLACOMBE – HAYTOR

Distance:	*Approx. 7 miles*
Time:	*Allow $3\frac{1}{2}$ – 4 hours*
Map:	*OS Outdoor Leisure 28*
Start reference:	*SX739792*
Terrain:	*Rough moorland paths; steep climbs*
Nearest town:	*Bovey Tracey*
Parking:	*Swallerton Gate*
Refreshments:	*Ice-cream vans, Swallerton Gate and Haytor car parks (April–September approx.)*

Hound Tor
Medieval Village
Becka Brook
Greator Rocks
Smallacombe Rocks
Holwell Quarry
tramway
Haytor Quarries
Haytor Rocks
Harefoot Cross
Saddle Tor
Seven Lords Lands
Hemsworthy Gate

Walk straight ahead to Hound Tor rocks, passing to the right-hand side of the Tor. As well as bracken and gorse, knotgrass and milkwort grow here, concealed in the cropped grass. As the path climbs, so the views open to Rippon and Saddle Tors. Follow the grassy path which leads away from Hound Tor; Greator Rocks are to the right with a splendid view left to Manaton.

Walk through the medieval village, partly concealed by bracken in the summer months, which lies between Hound Tor and Greator. It is easily found as many of the foundations of the houses still remain. This was a sizeable farming community from the 10th to the 14th century, and it is not certain why the village was abandoned. It may have been the Black Death, which was rampant in the 14th century, or perhaps it was the changing climate of the moor.

From the ruins, continue NE away from the village along the grassy track, and pass through a hunt gate to descend beside a larch plantation (L). Follow the path downwards to the

small stone bridge over the Becka Brook, from where the path winds its way amongst boulders and passes an old quarry, now overgrown with rowan trees. There are moss-covered boulders all around, as well as oak, hazel and hawthorn trees.

Beehive hut

Emerging from the trees, briefly bear left, then ascend the hill ahead, with Smallacombe Rocks to the right and Leighon Tor to the left. Looking back there are views to Greator Rocks and Hound Tor. Shortly turn right (S) to walk across the ridge formed by Smallacombe Rocks. To the east of the Rocks is a group of hut circles, over 3,000 years old. They were excavated in 1896, giving up fragments of pottery. Do not wander from the grassy path, as it will be noticed that to the right of it the ground is very wet and boggy; this area is

thick with rush and sphagnum mosses, both red and green. It is this moss which helps to form peat when the shoots die.

Ahead the sheer rock face of Holwell quarry can be seen rising above the spoil heaps, and a clear path leads towards the quarry and joins the granite tramway which once carried the granite produced by this quarry. Although long abandoned, a beehive hut once used by the workmen still survives amongst the granite clutter below the rock face.

Turn left along the tramway, which was the project of Mr George Templer. It was completed in 1820, and conveyed the granite to the Stover Canal (built by his father). This was quite an accomplishment as the terminus at the quarries is 1200 feet higher than the canal. Due to poor management of the quarries the tramway was abandoned in 1858, although excavation at the quarries continued intermittently until the 1880s, using other methods of transport for the granite.

Ignore the junction to the main line of the tramway, which comes in from the right, and continue to a second junction, where bear right towards the spoil heaps of Haytor quarry.

The tramway ceases, but follow the path towards Haytor Rocks, from where the views are magnificent; looking south are Tor Bay, Lyme Bay and the Channel and part of the Teign Estuary. To the east lies Haldon Hill with its recently restored Belvedere or Lawrence Tower, whilst the remainder of the view encompasses the vast moor.

Prior to the Rocks a small gate is passed to the right, from where a steep narrow path runs down to the quarry floor, which has now been reclaimed by nature, where dragonflies, newts and water lilies thrive in summer, and where even a kingfisher may be seen perching on the rusting winch left from the quarry's past.

Apart from providing the granite for the arches of London Bridge and for the columns of the British Museum Library, Haytor has also featured in films – in 1956 it was used in a scene for *Knights of the Round Table*, a British Film which starred Ava Gardner and Robert Taylor – and as might be expected has its legend too.

The story of the Lady's Leap dates from the late 1800s and arose from a daughter's defiance of her father, who wished her to marry for riches, but she preferred youth and poverty. She eventually agreed to marry her father's choice of husband, but insisted upon a breakfast being given for the wedding party, before the wedding, beneath Haytor Rocks. Whilst the party were enjoying the feast provided, the bride retreated to the summit of the tor, from where she apparently waved to them with her handkerchief. She sat for a short while then arose as if to return, but instead of descending, she spread her arms and leapt into space. Immediately, those who had observed this leap rushed around the tor, expecting to find her lying dead. What they saw was the daughter and her chosen youthful bridegroom, astride a horse speeding towards Widecombe, where they were swiftly married, much to the annoyance of her elderly suitor who had already settled several manors upon her!

Gradually descend, to follow a south-westerly course towards Saddle Tor, with Rippon Tor opposite. Pass beneath Saddle Tor, and continue alongside the road to reach Hemsworthy Gate.

Once through the gate, cross to the right of the road. Roughly 200 yards to the north of this gate, close to the enclosure wall, is a hut circle known as Seven Lord's Lands. It is so called as it marks the meeting point of seven manors.

There is now a convenient path to follow, running north-westwards, thus avoiding the road. Keep on this path until an enclosure wall is met, then rejoin the minor road.

Shortly after a cattle grid, a signpost on the right indicates a path to Houndtor Down and Haytor Down. After a short climb, Hound Tor can be used as a guide to return to Houndtor Down and the descent to Swallerton Gate.

HENNOCK RESERVOIRS – ELSFORD VIA WRAYLAND

Distance: *Approx. 6 miles*
Time: *Allow 4 – 4½ hours*
Map: *OS Outdoor Leisure 28*
Start reference: *SX805824*
Terrain: *Country lanes, woodland and field paths; steep climbs*
Nearest town: *Bovey Tracey*
Parking: *Car park at reservoirs (free)*
Refreshments: *The Cleave Inn and Primrose Cottage Tearooms, Lustleigh*

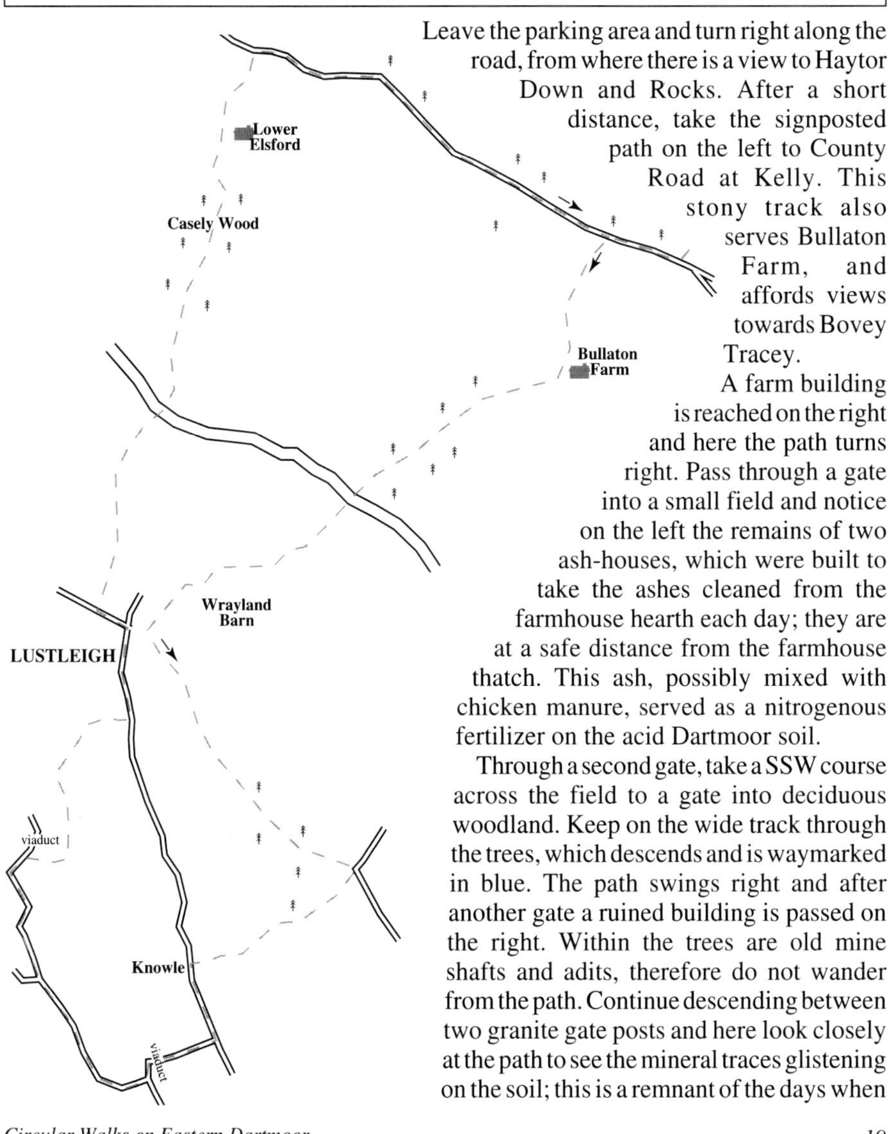

Leave the parking area and turn right along the road, from where there is a view to Haytor Down and Rocks. After a short distance, take the signposted path on the left to County Road at Kelly. This stony track also serves Bullaton Farm, and affords views towards Bovey Tracey.

A farm building is reached on the right and here the path turns right. Pass through a gate into a small field and notice on the left the remains of two ash-houses, which were built to take the ashes cleaned from the farmhouse hearth each day; they are at a safe distance from the farmhouse thatch. This ash, possibly mixed with chicken manure, served as a nitrogenous fertilizer on the acid Dartmoor soil.

Through a second gate, take a SSW course across the field to a gate into deciduous woodland. Keep on the wide track through the trees, which descends and is waymarked in blue. The path swings right and after another gate a ruined building is passed on the right. Within the trees are old mine shafts and adits, therefore do not wander from the path. Continue descending between two granite gate posts and here look closely at the path to see the mineral traces glistening on the soil; this is a remnant of the days when "shining ore" was mined at Kelly mine. This mine operated from the beginning of the 19th century until the mid-1950s.

When the road is reached, cross to join the public footpath to Lustleigh via Wrayland Barn; here again are splendid views to Trendlebere Down and Black Hill. At the far corner of the field cross a stile and stream into a second field and continue alongside the hedge to reach a ladder stile. Follow a roughly westerly course through this next field, which is a damp meadow and home to plants such as the ragged robin, soft rush, common knapweed, hairy tare, welted thistle and greater bird's-foot trefoil. A narrow path alongside a wall clothed in mosses and wall-pennywort is reached, which exits into a metalled lane.

Turn left along the route indicated to Hatherleigh, and soon the wide lane narrows to a grassy path. Climbing all the while, there are views on the left across the Wray valley. A stile takes the path into Higher Knowle Wood, a mixed woodland of oak, beech, holly, hazel and some conifers. Look into the trees to see the many nesting boxes, whilst the ground beneath the trees is massed with ferns and mosses. Follow the path through the trees to a gate and stile onto a narrow lane.

Turn immediately right onto the unmade track which passes alongside the woodland. Here there are hart's-tongue ferns in abundance as well as many fungi around the trees and dead stumps. Descend to a minor road, where turn left to pass between walls and high hedges and beside the grounds of Knowle, wherein grows a fine blue-green Atlas Cedar.

At a junction in the road bear right to Manaton, indicated by a very ancient signpost. This narrow road descends and passes beneath a viaduct which once carried the railway line from Newton Abbot to Moretonhampstead.

This line was begun in August 1863 and completed in 1866, with its first complete run being on 4th July. It was built by the then Moretonhampstead and South Devon Railways, involving a capital outlay of £105,000. It was twelve miles long and passed through Heathfield, Teigngrace, Bovey Tracey and Lustleigh. On 1st July 1872, South Devon Railways was amalgamated with the Great Western Railway, which in turn was amalgamated into British Railways on 31st December 1947. Once eleven trains a day, with six as far as Bovey Tracey, used this line. The last train ran on 2nd March 1959.

Cross a small bridge over a tributary to the River Bovey, then turn right along the road indicated to Rudge and Sandusk. The road, bordered by hedgerows colourful with foxgloves, campion, wild strawberries and hogweed, climbs steadily, and below to the right is the dismantled railway line. When a fork in the road is reached, bear right and shortly take the path on the right leading to Wrayland. Descend between the stone pillars of a now-dismantled railway bridge to follow the grassy path through the Water Treatment Works and cross the Wray Brook by means of a small footbridge.

Lustleigh

Once more the path enters a wooded area; when a grassy clearing is reached on the left, walk through the trees to view a magnificent 41-foot-high viaduct, which is rapidly being overtaken by nature. On the boulders around are fine examples of fir clubmoss, sedum and common hair moss, as well as polypody ferns.

A gate takes the path into a field, where keep alongside the right-hand hedge. Through another gate go straight ahead to a lane and turn left. This leads to a minor road, where turn right and at the next junction, follow the road to Lustleigh.

A line of cottages is passed on the right and ahead is a railway bridge. (To visit Lustleigh for refreshments, continue over the bridge and follow the road into the village.) Before reaching the bridge, turn right into a field and walk straight ahead to cross a small footbridge. Bear left and continue in a northerly direction across the field to a stile in the

hedgerow. Look to the left to see concrete steps and a pipe-line; this pipe carries water from the reservoir at Fernworthy to the Lower Tottiford Reservoir, one of the three Hennock Reservoirs. Keep on the same course across this next field towards the road. A bar stile in the wall gives access to the main road (A382).

Cross the road to take the signposted footpath opposite to County Road via Elsford. A steady climb along a boulder-strewn path emerges into a field, from where there is a view back to Lustleigh and beyond. Take a NNE course to the trees ahead – Casely Wood. The narrow woodland path climbs quite steeply and is wet in places. In this habitat will be found woody nightshade, wood avens, dog's mercury, primroses, yellow pimpernel, common cow-wheat and golden saxifrage.

Emerging onto a wide stony track, bear right to follow the track past Elsford Cottage and join a minor road. Turn right and climb again. There are fine views through gateways along the way – Haytor Rocks being clearly seen on the horizon. Continue on this road to return to Bullaton Cross and the car park.

LUSTLEIGH – PETHYBRIDGE VIA HAMMERSLAKE AND FOXWORTHY

Distance:	*Approx. 6 miles*
Time:	*Allow 4 – 4½ hours*
Map:	*OS Outdoor Leisure 28*
Start reference:	*SX 785814*
Terrain:	*Stony woodland paths, tracks and country lanes; steep climbs*
Nearest town:	*Bovey Tracey*
Parking:	*Limited parking in village*
Refreshments:	*The Cleave Inn and Primrose Cottage Tearooms, Lustleigh*

Locate the road (L) just above the church where the War Memorial stands. Walk up this road for a few yards to bear left onto the signposted footpath to the Cleave. This stony track passes between properties and enters a field via a small kissing gate. Walk across this field (NW) to another kissing-gate and keep the same course through the next field, walking towards a clump of trees.

Through a gate the path becomes narrow and is bordered by hazel, holly, elder and oak trees, as well as wild flowers such as dog's mercury, campion, hedge woundwort, hedge mustard, foxgloves and wall-pennywort in season.

When a minor lane is reached, turn left to Hammerslake keeping alongside the cottages to go straight ahead through a gate (waymarked) onto a narrow path through woodland. Cross a small clapper bridge and the way bears left and begins climbing through scattered granite boulders and a woodland floor populated by hart's-tongue ferns, pink purslane, wood avens, wall-pennywort and Indian balsam. Leave the woods via a stile onto a narrow country lane.

Turn left and very shortly turn right up a path indicated 'Hunter's Tor 1¼ m'. Pass through a gate at the top of this narrow path and keep straight ahead.

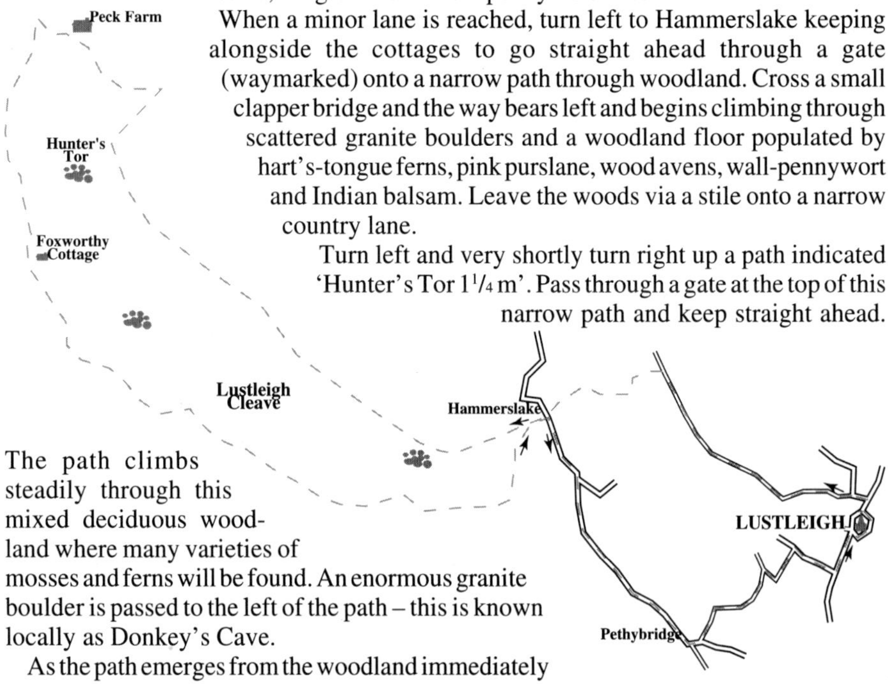

The path climbs steadily through this mixed deciduous woodland where many varieties of mosses and ferns will be found. An enormous granite boulder is passed to the left of the path – this is known locally as Donkey's Cave.

As the path emerges from the woodland immediately there is a view to Hound Tor. From the ridge further splendid views open up – in the valley pick out the church at Manaton. This wide grassy track leads to Hunter's Tor, the granite pile at the far end of the ridge; growing in the short grass along this ridge are thyme-leaved speedwell and knotweed, both bearing very minute, delicate flowers in season. Although not readily recognisable, there is an ancient Iron Age hill fort just prior to reaching Hunter's Tor, one of a number of encampments above the gorge of the Teign. The path passes through this hill fort, which is now just a series of shallow ditches and low stone walls.

On reaching Hunter's Tor, pause to soak up the panoramic views from here – from left to right there are Haytor Rocks, Rippon Tor, Greator Rocks (a little below the horizon) and Hound Tor. Next comes Hayne Down with Bowerman's Nose protruding from its side, then Easdon Down, and further round North Bovey church is seen together with the Manor House Hotel.

Leave the Tor and follow the path downhill (NE), keeping the wall to the right. The path turns sharp left and descends a stony track to Peck Farm, from where follow the farm track to a point where the way divides.

Turn left through a gate onto a track indicated to Foxworthy Bridge. This path is lined by sycamore, birch and hazel, with both pale and rosebay willowherb, and foxgloves, giving a cheerful splash of colour when in bloom, as well as attracting butterflies such as the speckled wood and skipper. Pass Foxworthy Cottage and take the path to Horsham Steps (SE); once more enter woodland.

Pass a sign indicating Horsham Steps to the right and continue towards Hammerslake. This pleasant path twists and turns, climbs and descends, and during the summer months may be engulfed by bracken. Occasionally there are breaks in the trees which provide an opportunity to enjoy the spectacular views.

When Hammerslake is reached, turn right through the gate to descend to the road, turning right along this quiet lane. Turn left at Pethybridge (opposite a property named Cleavelands St Mary) and take the next lane on the right between cottages to arrive at a T-junction, from where there is a splendid view over Lustleigh village.

Turn right to descend, passing the Baptist Church (L); at the next junction turn left and walk towards the village centre. Turn right to pass the church and visit the tearooms.

Lustleigh was home to the Reverend William Davy for over 40 years. He founded a school here in 1825, which still stands in the churchyard. During his time here he completed a life-time's work, which he entitled a *System of Divinity*. It consisted of 26 volumes of 500 pages each. When completed, he presented a copy to his Bishop, who allegedly remarked that he could "not be supposed to notice every trifle that appears in print", to which Davy is reputed to have replied, "If your Lordship considers twenty-six volumes of 8vo, the labour of fifty years in collecting, compiling and printing, to be a trifle, I most certainly cannot allow myself to expect from your Lordship either approbation or encouragement". On his retirement from Lustleigh, Davy settled on a small farm called Willmead, where he became an accomplished gardener and collector of rare plants. At the age of 82 he was presented to the living of Winkleigh, which removed him from his treasured garden and encumbered him with a damp vicarage. He died after holding the benefice for just five months, having caught a chill following the move.

WIDECOMBE – HAMEL DOWN – RAF MEMORIAL – NATSWORTHY

Distance:	*Approx. 7 miles*
Time:	*Allow $3\frac{1}{2}$ – 4 hours*
Map:	*OS Outdoor Leisure 28*
Start reference:	*SX719768*
Terrain:	*Rough tracks, moorland and country lanes; some climbs*
Nearest town:	*Ashburton*
Parking:	*Car park, Widecombe*
Refreshments:	*Rugglestone Inn and Old Inn, Widecombe*

From the car park turn right alongside the green to reach the junction with the minor road to Natsworthy. Go right again along this road and shortly turn left up Church Lane, a metalled track signposted Hamel Down for Grimspound.

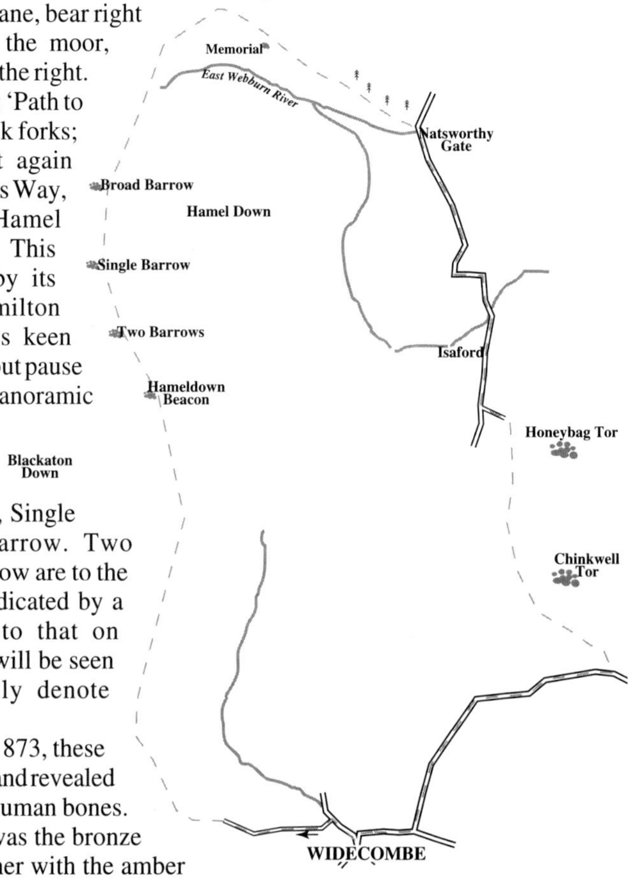

At the end of Church Lane, bear right (NNW) up the side of the moor, keeping the stone wall to the right. A sign is passed denoting 'Path to Widecombe' and the track forks; here bear slightly right again (NW) onto the Two Moors Way, leading to the top of Hamel Down and its Beacon. This Beacon is announced by its granite marker as Hamilton Beacon and the wind is keen here even on a calm day, but pause briefly to appreciate the panoramic views on offer.

From Hameldown Beacon, the next landmarks are Two Barrows, Single Barrow and Broad Barrow. Two Barrows and Single Barrow are to the left of the path, each indicated by a stone marker similar to that on Hameldown Beacon. It will be seen that the stones actually denote Burrows not Barrows.

In the years 1872 and 1873, these Barrows were excavated and revealed small amounts of burnt human bones. The most exciting find was the bronze blade of a dagger, together with the amber pommel inlaid with gold. From this lofty elevation there are few prominent heights within the Dartmoor region that cannot be seen. It is possible to see Dartmoor's three forestry plantations – Bellever, Soussons and Fernworthy (left to right).

Broad Barrow is seen ahead on the horizon; pass to its right (NE). The wonderful views continue and away to the left can be seen the trig point on Hameldown Tor (the highest point on Hamel Down). This well-defined track veers to the right and the plantation at Heathercombe is seen.

The path descends gradually to pass the RAF memorial, which was set up here to commemorate the crew of a bomber from 49 Squadron, Scampton, which crashed returning from a mission over France, on 21st March 1941. The large granite memorial is engraved with the initials of the four crew – R.D.W, C.J.L, R.B. and R.L.A.E. It also bears a plaque, affixed in 1991, from the Aircrew Association.

From here there are more expansive views – Moretonhampstead with Easdon Tor to the right and to the left Castle Drogo. As the path descends so the tors of Honeybag, Chinkwell, Hound Tor, Haytor and Rippon Tor can all be identified.

Descend the bracken covered hill (ENE) to take the path alongside the Heathercombe plantation. The wall enclosing these trees is massed with lichen and moss; they tumble over one another, combining to make a superb natural cushion on the granite.

Follow the path to Natsworthy gate and turn right down the road towards Widecombe. After about three quarters of a mile a cattle grid is reached, shortly after Isaford Farm. From here there is a choice of route – either continue on down this narrow, but fairly quiet, lane which leads directly back to Widecombe, or immediately after this grid, turn left (ESE) and climb the rough steep track to a gate. This is Thorneyhill Lane, which runs beside a conifer plantation and below Honeybag and Chinkwell Tors. This lane exits onto a road just below Bonehill Rocks.

Where this lane rejoins the road turn right between stone gateposts and descend to a small bridge over the East Webburn River. At the T-junction turn right and return to Widecombe.

Apart from its September Fair, Widecombe's other best known feature is its large perpendicular style church, which has gained the title 'Cathedral of the Moor'. The tower serves as a landmark for miles around, standing 120 feet high, and topped by four pinnacles supporting four crosses. It suffered considerable damage when it was struck by lightning on 21st October 1638, during a service; four were killed and many died later from their injuries. The village schoolmaster of the day recorded this incident and his account may be seen mounted on boards within the church.

The Dartmoor authoress Beatrice Chase (Olive Katharine Parr) is buried within this churchyard. She lived at nearby Venton House for over 50 years. Her memorial cross bears the inscription 'Pray for Olive Katharine Parr' on the one side and 'Beatrice Chase 1874–1955' on the other.

DARTMEET – DOLLY'S COT – LAUGHTER HOLE

Distance:	*Approx. 6½ miles*
Time:	*Allow 4½ – 5 hours*
Map:	*OS Outdoor Leisure 28*
Start reference:	*SX672732*
Terrain:	*Field paths, stony tracks, rough moorland; wet and boggy in places*
Nearest town:	*Ashburton*
Parking:	*Dartmeet car park (privately managed by the owners of Badgers' Holt for their patrons and the general public)*
Refreshments:	*Badgers' Holt, Dartmeet; Brimpts Farm*

Return to the road and turn right across the bridge, immediately turning left onto the signposted footpath to Huccaby, which is waymarked in yellow. Follow the path upwards through the field to a stony track between walls elegantly clothed in mosses and pennywort. As the track climbs the banks become colourful with sheep's bit scabious, foxgloves, pennywort, and swathes of bracken; hawthorn, rowan and sycamore grow alongside the track.

Emerging into a field there are splendid views towards Hexworthy, Sherberton and Down Ridge. Through a gate near farm buildings turn right along a minor road. Here the verges are massed with yarrow, both pink and white, tormentil, greater bird's-foot trefoil and white clover.

At the T-junction, turn right along the well-used road. When the Forestry Commission land at Brimpts is reached on the left, follow the signposted bridlepath, passing beneath an avenue of beech trees. Pass in front of Brimpts farmhouse and through a gate bear left, then right to a gate beside a cottage. Here the path is signposted again. Keep on the well defined path through the fields and soon the ruin of Dolly's Cot is seen on the left of the track.

There is now only one wall left standing, that with the chimney. The two fireplaces remain, but they are now taken over by ferns and other vegetation. The story attaches to this ruined cottage that it was built by a gentleman for his newly-wedded wife Dolly, whom he wished to remove from those who admired her rather more than he cared for. This was at a time when Sir Thomas Tyrwhitt (d. 1831), who was responsible for the building of Princetown Prison and much of that settlement, owned the Tor Royal at Princetown and held many bachelor parties. It appears that some of his guests at these parties were attracted to this lady and there were even rumours that King George IV, who was a friend of Tyrwhitt, was one of these admirers. However, the story remains

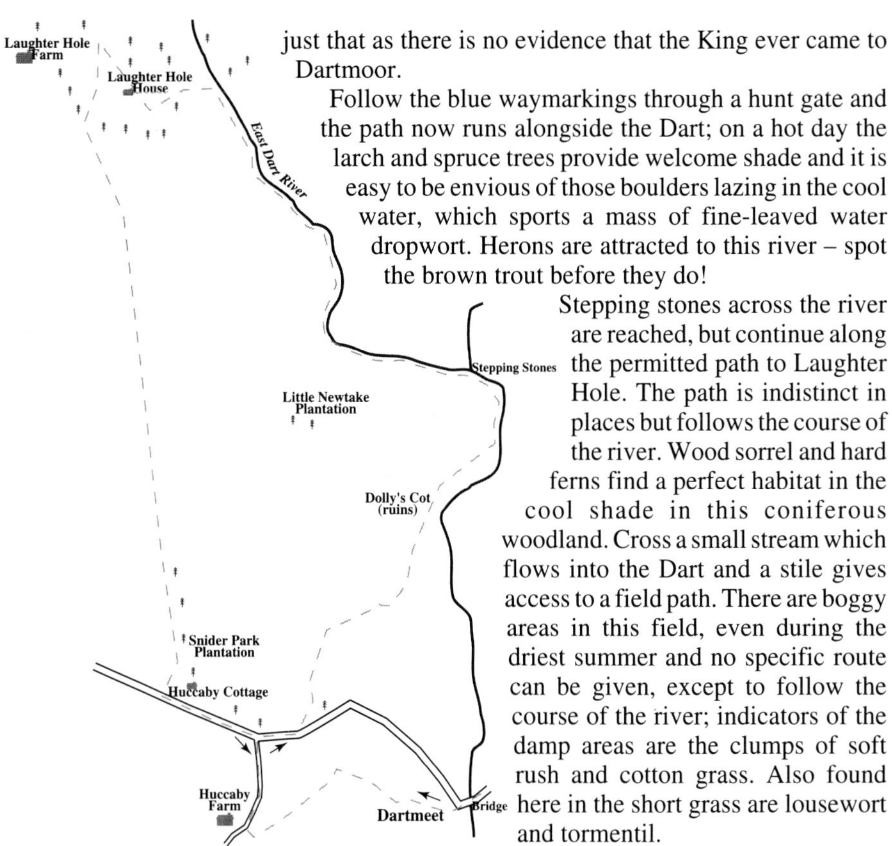

just that as there is no evidence that the King ever came to Dartmoor.

Follow the blue waymarkings through a hunt gate and the path now runs alongside the Dart; on a hot day the larch and spruce trees provide welcome shade and it is easy to be envious of those boulders lazing in the cool water, which sports a mass of fine-leaved water dropwort. Herons are attracted to this river – spot the brown trout before they do!

Stepping stones across the river are reached, but continue along the permitted path to Laughter Hole. The path is indistinct in places but follows the course of the river. Wood sorrel and hard ferns find a perfect habitat in the cool shade in this coniferous woodland. Cross a small stream which flows into the Dart and a stile gives access to a field path. There are boggy areas in this field, even during the driest summer and no specific route can be given, except to follow the course of the river; indicators of the damp areas are the clumps of soft rush and cotton grass. Also found here in the short grass are lousewort and tormentil.

When Laughter Hole House comes into view, an enclosure wall will be seen and here there is a ladder stile and another signpost. Turn left to follow the path uphill, and then turn right where indicated. From here views begin to open up and Riddon Ridge is unmistakeable. Turn sharp left to pass Laughter Hole Farm and follow the track to Huccaby Cottage. At the top of this stony track, a seat has been thoughtfully provided, giving an opportunity to savour the view. Yar Tor, Corndon Tor and Down as well as Riddon Ridge are seen.

Pass through the hunt gate and follow the path indicated to Huccaby. Don't descend into the dip as this appears to be wet, but keep along the high ground, correcting the course to south along the way. From this height Laughter Tor (a corruption of Lough Tor), together with its standing stone, Sharp Tor and North Hessary Tor, with its television mast, are all seen.

When Little Newtake and Snider Park plantations come into view, use these as a guide to arrive at another hunt gate and signpost. Follow the path alongside the plantation to arrive at a gate onto the B3357, Dartmeet to Princetown Road.

Turn left and with care walk along the road to return to the lane to Hexworthy. Turn right here and follow the road down to the farm track (L) at Huccaby Farm. Follow the yellow waymarkings to return along the outward route. On this return route, the road winding its way down to Dartmeet stands out clearly, as does the great expanse of Corndon Down.

BEL TOR CORNER – CORNDON TOR – PONSWORTHY

Distance:	*Approx. 5½ miles*
Time:	*Allow 3 – 3½ hours*
Map:	*OS Outdoor Leisure 28*
Start reference:	*SX696732*
Terrain:	*Field paths, moorland and country lanes; several climbs*
Nearest town:	*Ashburton*
Parking:	*Bel Tor Corner*

From the parking area, turn left along the roadside and follow the road until a wide track is reached on the right. Take this track across the open moorland, with Corndon Down and Tor looming large ahead. Cross the minor road and continue along the wide track through the gorse and bracken to arrive at the summit of Corndon Tor.

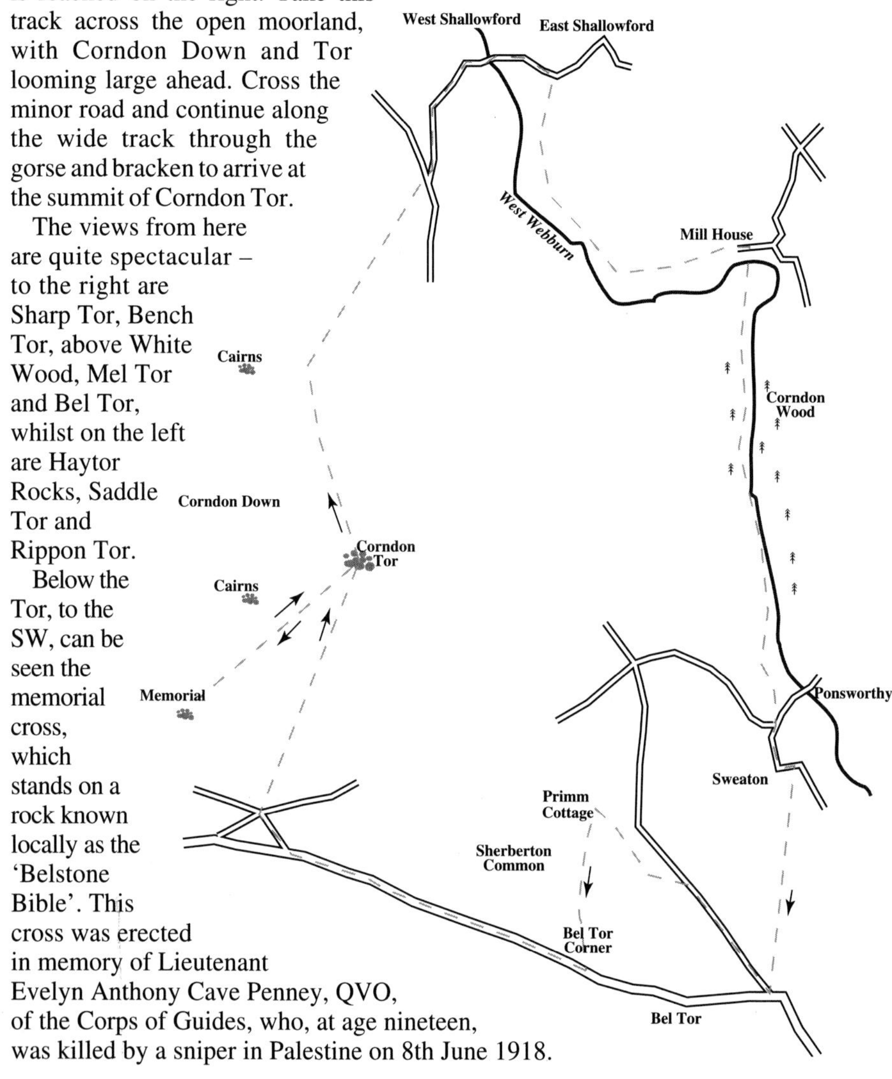

The views from here are quite spectacular – to the right are Sharp Tor, Bench Tor, above White Wood, Mel Tor and Bel Tor, whilst on the left are Haytor Rocks, Saddle Tor and Rippon Tor.

Below the Tor, to the SW, can be seen the memorial cross, which stands on a rock known locally as the 'Belstone Bible'. This cross was erected in memory of Lieutenant Evelyn Anthony Cave Penney, QVO, of the Corps of Guides, who, at age nineteen, was killed by a sniper in Palestine on 8th June 1918.

Take a northerly course from the Tor, along a wide stony track, making for two large cairns (ancient burial places). There are several cairns on Corndon Down, the largest of which, having a diameter of 120 feet, will be passed to the left of this track. On the descent from these cairns, there are more splendid views – Bellever Tor can be picked out to the left.

The heather, gorse and bilberry make a colourful carpet to the moor and, of course, there are the melodious calls of the larks, pipits and other moorland birds to provide a pleasant accompaniment to the walk.

The track joins a minor road and immediately opposite should be the narrow lane leading to Shallowford. Follow this lane, shortly crossing the West Webburn River, and as it begins to climb, take the signposted bridle-path on the right, indicated to County Road, Jordan. The path is quite clear and provides easy walking alongside the Webburn.

When the path emerges alongside Mill House and Jordan Cottage, turn sharp right to descend past Jordan Cottage and cross the West Webburn via a wooden footbridge. Bear left over the bridge and continue alongside the river. The bracken will be high during the summer months and obscure any vision of the water. However, when the path enters woodland, the way becomes clearer and careful observation in the river will reveal brown trout enjoying the cool clear water.

A slip-bar gate signals a change of surroundings and the path enters a field, shortly exiting onto the road at Forder Bridge Cross, Ponsworthy. Bear right along the road indicated to Ashburton and climb to Sweaton Farm on the right. Turn into the farm entrance and follow the signposted path southwards up a stony track. In the field, continue in the same direction alongside the hedge to arrive at a stile; keep the same course to reach a second stile onto a minor lane.

Bear right and follow the lane until a wide track is reached on the left, leading onto Sherberton Common; shortly Primm Cottage is passed on the left and now bear left (S) to continue on a wide grassy track back to Bel Tor Corner.

ILSINGTON – HAYTOR VALE

Distance:	*Approx. 4 miles*
Time:	*Allow 2½ – 3 hours*
Map:	*OS Outdoor Leisure 28*
Start reference:	*SX785763*
Terrain:	*Stony tracks and quiet country lanes; some steep climbs*
Nearest town:	*Bovey Tracey*
Parking:	*Near church*
Refreshments:	*The Carpenter's Arms, Ilsington; The Rock Inn, Haytor Vale*

Join the road leading westwards towards Haytor and after a short distance take the turning on the right signposted to Trumpeter. This quiet lane is bordered by a mix of oak, holly, birch and sycamore with the banks being home to many wild flowers, including green alkanet, foxgloves, pink purslane, campion and stitchwort, as well as honeysuckle and black bryony in season.

There are good views away to the right of this lane and a glimpse of Saddle Tor is gained as the road descends slightly. Arriving at Trumpeter, follow the road past several properties until a Public Path sign is seen on the left, denoting the Moor three quarters of a mile and Haytor Vale one mile; this track also leads to Smallacombe Farm and Stables. At the stables, pass between the farm buildings, through a gate, then follow the path indicated to the right and climb quite steeply along a stony track. This climb rewards with a wonderful view over the valley and Ilsington church is clearly seen.

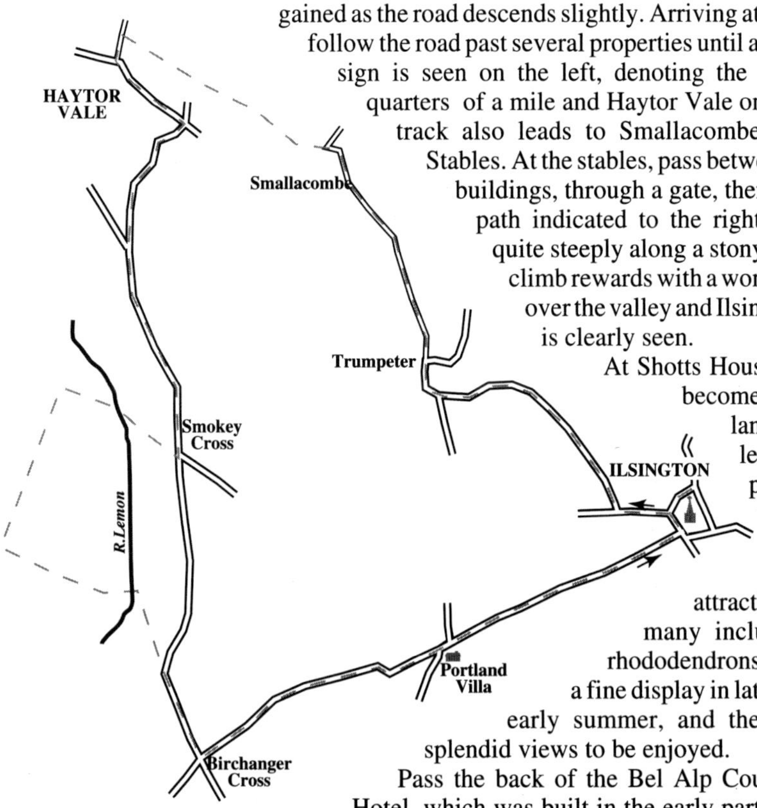

At Shotts House, the track becomes a metalled lane; here turn left. The way passes between large properties with most attractive gardens, many including large rhododendrons, which give a fine display in late spring and early summer, and there are also splendid views to be enjoyed.

Pass the back of the Bel Alp Country House Hotel, which was built in the early part of the 20th century for the tobacco heiress, Dame Violet Wills, and go through a turnstile into woodland. Keep on the path heading west, following it until it joins a metalled lane; turn left to emerge onto a minor road, where turn left again to the village of Haytor Vale.

Although there was a farming community in this area from as early as the 13th century, the village of Haytor Vale did not become established until early in the 19th century, as a direct result of the quarrying on Haytor Down.

Pass the Post Office and the Rock Inn, once a hostelry for the quarrymen, and after a short distance a junction is reached. Bear left along the road, passing Pinchaford to the right; to the right Saddle Tor and Bagtor Down are visible.

When Smokey Cross is reached, turn sharp right along a track signposted 'Public Bridlepath'. There are properties at the end of this undulating track so be prepared for traffic. At the top of the track, pass through a gate onto the foot of Bagtor Down and turn left, keeping the wall left. Walk through the bracken, gorse and sheep until a signposted Public Bridlepath leading ESE is reached on the left. Pass through the gate and onto a narrow path, where again the way is edged by masses of wild flowers, with pink purslane, cranesbill, herb robert, foxgloves, bluebells, lesser celandines and stitchwort putting on a colourful show when in bloom.

The path is stony and damp in places, giving a foothold to ferns such as the shuttlecock and hart's tongue. Passing through a small wooded area, the path briefly runs alongside the River Lemon, wherein grows fine-leaved water dropwort. Cross the river via a small footbridge and climb through mixed woodland, where wood sanicle, violets and speedwell thrive.

Where the path emerges onto a minor road, bear right and continue to Birchanger Cross. Turn left (NE) here and walk along this narrow lane with high hedgerows, full of wild flowers. The hedges are a mix of holly, small-leaved lime and sycamore, draped with honeysuckle. Pass the Methodist Church and at the T-junction, bear left and keep straight on to pass Portland Villa on the right. This road leads into Ilsington village, where it ends at a T-junction.

If time allows, visit the church, with which John Ford the dramatist is associated; turn left along the road for a few yards to the lych gate with a small room above. This is a modern structure, replacing a dilapidated building which was taken down in 1871. Prior to this, there was a schoolroom over the west gate, which collapsed in 1639. At the time, the master and seventeen schoolboys were within, but fortunately none suffered serious injury.

In January 1646, following their defeat at Bovey Tracey, Royalist soldiers retreated to Ilsington, seeking refuge in the church, but they were pursued by Cromwell's men and forced to leave the building.

Entrance to the church is through the south porch, with sun-dial over, above which is a Priest's room reached by a stairway inside the church. The church dates from the late 15th century, although much of the interior has been restored. However, the wagon roofs are of interest, displaying several carved bosses; one of which is the three rabbits with conjoined ears – the tinners' symbol. There are a number of tombstones, dating from the 17th century, set into the floor, and a memorial stone to a member of the Ford family will be found near the choir stalls, although much of the inscription upon it has become illegible. The stained glass windows are few, but that in the south transept to John and Henrietta Divett (1888) is particularly striking. John Divett built the 'Old Mill' at Bovey Tracey in 1854 as stabling and outhouses for his private house 'Riverside'.

On the west wall is a memorial to Jane Ford, daughter of Thomas Ford of Bagtor. John Ford (1586–1639), was born at Bagtor House and christened in this church. He attended Exeter College, matriculating in 1601. In 1606 he wrote the elegy 'Fame's Memorial' or 'The Earl of Devonshire Deceased', which he dedicated to the Earl's widow, the former Lady Rich, but his career as a dramatist did not begin until 1623. Then, together with William Rowley and Thomas Dekker, he wrote *The Witch of Edmonton*; in 1624 he collaborated with Dekker to write *The Sun's Darling*. His first stage presentation was *The Lover's Melancholy* (1629) and he produced further plays in 1633, 1634 and 1639. The date of his death is thought to be 1639, but his burial place is unknown.

A walk around the churchyard reveals a tombstone to Thomas Ford close to the SE corner of the chancel wall, and remains of the ancient Manor House which once stood in the NE part of the churchyard. It was abandoned in the 17th century and eventually pulled down in the 1870s. Careful observation is required to discover the carved stones which once adorned the mullion windows.